AMERICAN PRIMITIVES

and

The People Who Used Them

Primitive America!

The frontiers of this great land were settled by nearly every nationality. People coming from nations all over the world, brave women and men, crossed the wide Missouri, canoed down the winding Snake, rafted up and down the Rogue, the Mississippi, the Ohio, and the Clinch rivers.

Through the Cumberland Gap out of the Valley of the Tennessee they came, riding, walking, carrying on their backs what they needed to hack homes out of the wilderness which stretched 2,000 miles or more across what was to become a great nation.

Across the granite hills of Vermont, down the valley of the Connecticut to the Hudson River, the sounds of their axes echoed across the land. In every part of this land we call our own, the hardy pioneers were building and creating, using the strength of their backs and the wisdom of their minds, trusting in God but keeping a tight hold on their rifles every step of the way.

"In God we trust!"

If the pioneers prayed hard, they worked twice as hard, toiling long hours on the trail, doing backbreaking labor to erect the crudest of dwellings to protect their families and livestock from the elements. It was a harsh land they were challenging. Many died before they accomplished what they set out to do. In working, and in dying, those whom we refer to as pioneers extended the different frontiers and joined them together into what we today proudly call the United States of America.

Illumined by half truths, the frontiers were mystic lands. There were few maps to go by, mostly rumors. When the pioneer survived, it was because he used his courage and his God-given skills to see him through, skills brought from the "old country," skills used not as a hobby, but for survival.

Whatever they needed, they created from the iron in the earth,

3

from the wool of the sheep, from the hides of every animal, from the virgin timber that covered much of the land.

"My boots and rifle saw me through!" was a common expression on the frontiers. When someone exclaimed, "He died with his boots on!" he meant just that. They slept in their boots, not knowing when they'd have to rise from their blankets to fight or deal with some emergency.

The pioneer always referred to his long rifle as "she." Betsy brought down a fine deer today. Sarah misfired, dammit!

The life of the pioneer varied but little no matter where he chose to "put down his roots." Survival was survival. If the pioneer's accent was Scottish, Jewish or had an English twang, he went about worshipping God in his own way, always pushing onward to the promised land.

"Open up the frontiers. Pass your know-how on to your next of kin. Pray to God for good weather, good crops, healthy children, and a strong woman to help in the fields and keep the cabin warm."

If you wonder where you got the grit to carry on when everything seemed lost, or if you wanted to quit but didn't, you probably inherited your backbone from your ancestors. You can walk a little taller and a little straighter because your Uncle Simon on your mother's grandfather's side "stood" at the Alamo in '36 or fought against the British at New Orleans with Andy Jackson and his Kentucky and Tennessee volunteers.

I'll say it for us all: God Bless America!

CONTENTS

American Primitives

by

Robert W. Miller

Published in the United States of America by
WALLACE-HOMESTEAD BOOK CO.
P.O. Box BI
Des Moines, Iowa 50304
Printed in U.S.A.

The Museum of Appalachia

His life was gentle, and the elements
so mix'd in him that Nature might stand up
and say to all the world, "This was a man!" — Shakespeare

Those fortunate enough to own a copy of the book, "The Story of Marcellus Moss Rice and His Big Valley Kinsman," written by a loving grandson, need only read the above quotation to know that John Rice Irwin, proprietor of the Museum of Appalachia, adored his grandfather, Marcellus Moss Rice.

Five hundred mile trips down the treacherous Clinch and Tennessee rivers on a log raft, coal mining in the distant Cumberland Mountains, hair-raising adventures in the Indian Territory, and a stint as a soldier in the south and Puerto Rico were but a few of the everyday experiences that John's grandfather had as he grew from boy to man.

One gets a view of the life of the pioneer just by reading John Rice Irwin's loving tale about his grandfather.

A chat with John, himself, makes you immediately aware that here is a man who stands tall alongside his ancestors. The strong conviction that his share in America's heritage should be preserved at any cost started this soft-spoken man on his way to collecting thousands of primitives, a "loving journey" that started some 30 years ago.

Encouraged by his grandfather and driven by a force that even today is unexplainable to John, he thought little of hiking twenty miles over mountain paths and unpaved roads to seek out a choice "primitive." After a time, other relatives joined with John, giving mostly "encouragement."

Some 30 years ago, John Rice Irwin began to beg, borrow and, well, add to his growing collection, which today is one of the largest and finest collections of primitives in America. Actually, if John Rice "stole" anything, it was a nip from a clay jug and then only because it was twenty below and there were two feet of snow on the ground.

Because he had a family to support, the Museum of Appalachia had to come second. Sometimes it was a choice of food on the table or buying another primitive. The Irwins never starved but to hear Liz, John's attractive wife, tell it, the wolf was not only at the front door but at the back door and climbing in five windows at the same time!

Slowly the museum took form — a new cabin here, split rail fences all around the property, and even the addition of a Mexican burro named Twinkles.

As the years passed — almost as if John's grandfather's hand were guiding the project — the museum grew, and grew, and grew. Working on weekends, long into the night, going into the mountains when the temperature was well below zero, pushing himself beyond the point that would put most men in the cemetery, John continued to build and collect. Sometimes his family and friends wouldn't see him for days. They knew John was trudging the mountain paths in search of a primitive that no other collector had.

Forty miles back in the wilderness where there were no roads, John would buy a hog scalding trough, carved from the trunk of a poplar tree and weighing at least 300 pounds. Somehow, some way, the trough ended up at John's museum. "John's Folly," the natives called it.

And then, almost as if John's grandfather had said, "It's ready, boy!" it was. There was still lots to be added and many things to be done, but the Museum of Appalachia was finally opened to the public.

John has been successful as a cemetery owner, musician (he plays 30 different stringed instruments), elementary and high school teacher and principal, college professor, author, newspaper reporter, drive-in restaurant owner, farmer, real estate promoter, historian, member of the county court, Sunday school teacher, and, at present, Director of the Tennessee Appalachia Educational Co-Operative, a group of dedicated people intent on improving the lives and living conditions of the impoverished mountain people who live in the vast Appalachian region.

The Museum of Appalachia is a collection of primitives used by the pioneers who settled in that region hundreds of years ago, but we should remember these same primitives were used on all the frontiers. John Rice Irwin has traveled the length and breadth of this country and discovered that what his ancestors used in the Big Valley was also used to settle New England, the Far West and the Deep South.

Even though the Museum of Appalachia is geographically located in Norris, Tennessee, the contents of the many buildings tell the story of American pioneers everywhere.

Taking no bows, standing quietly in the background, John Rice Irwin says to all who listen: "I hold the strong conviction that the true breed of mountain folk of Appalachia, and the ancestors of those who pioneered this great land of ours are among the most admirable people in the world. Abounding in gentle kindness and compassion, these brave people will forever be remembered by those who truly believe in America. I consider it a privilege to be a citizen of the most beautiful land in the world."

To those of you who also believe in the heritage of America, what more can be said!

The Pioneer Household

★ A beautiful butter mold and two small "patty" molds. Life was a chore, and anything that added the least bit of joy to the household was used at the dining room table. These items date back to the late 1700s, going out of vogue in the early 20th century, though they are still used in certain isolated areas today.

★ Everyone loved popcorn, even back in the early 1800s. This type was used over a fire on the hearth.

★ Pucker up! This is an early lemon squeezer. It worked!

★ No need to tell you what this is! Materials have changed through the years, but its multiple uses are still with us.

★ An early American butter churn, complete with lid and dasher. The housewife made butter by putting cream in the wooden churn, then dashing up and down with the long rod. It was good butter too! Early 1800s.

9

★ This crude utensil box kept the knives and forks on the wall when not in use. Early 1800s.

★ A typical earthenware jug, used for carrying water, sorghum, or whatever. "Hand thrown" at the hearth, it wasn't particularly pretty but it served its purpose. Early 1800s.

★ This is a crude coffee grinder. The nut on top of the cup could be adjusted to regulate the bean "grind."

★ This factory-made gadget from around the time of the Civil War was used to remove the pits from cherries. It still works today!

★ This small castiron pot-on-legs was used to heat water for making coffee or for shaving. Placed on the hearth, it did the trick in the days before the wood-burning stove.

★ One of the earliest known cabbage cutters, it dates back to the late 1700s. Also used for cutting curd.

★ This brass kettle, used for many purposes, dates back to the early 1800s.

★ This "decorative" item was made from the hair of a cow's or horse's tail. It hung in the kitchen of the early settlement homes, and probably was the forerunner of today's fly swatter. More of a swisher than a swatter, it nevertheless did the job!

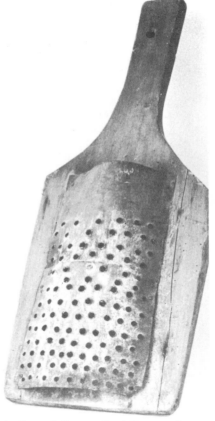

★ This Early American wooden bottle was carried into the field by farmers in the mid-1800s.

★ One of the earliest forms of corn graters, it goes back to the days of Daniel Boone.

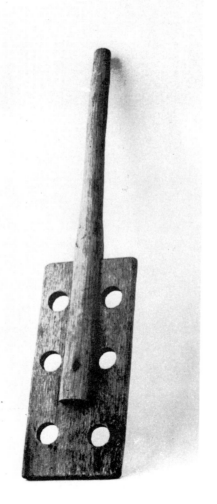

★ Called a "battling stick," this was used for washing clothes in the early 1800s.

★ This is an Early American cloth stretcher, used to stretch the cloth after it was removed from the loom.

★ This lamp is of the kerosene type, indicating it was made after 1850.

★ Andirons or "fire dogs" have been around since the first home fires were built in America. This crude-looking pair was obviously hand-forged for use in a farmhouse. Around 1840.

★ Without this gadget, you'd have frozen to death in the days of the pioneer. Fires, left "banked" at night, had to be brought to life in the early morning in time for father to shave, if he were going to Sunday meeting. The bellows did just that — they "roared" at the flames — thus the name.

16

★ This is how the pioneers stored their strips of white oak. Came the winter, Ma busied herself with the making of baskets for many purposes.

★ A hand-woven basket from split oak strips, its contents are sassafras roots for making tea. The basket was also used for gathering eggs, and many other things.

17

★ This is a broom press. The broom corn was placed in the rack, tightened down to the peg holes, then sewn together with hemp. Then the handle was added.

★ This vicious-looking tool is a hetchel and was used to remove the outside husk from the flax plant. You knelt on the pads at either end and pulled the flax stalks toward you. It was no work for a boy! Early 1800s.

★ This double cruisie (Phoebe lamp) Betty lamps goes back to the earliest days of the American colonists. Animal fat was used as "fuel" and, at best, it didn't give off too much light.

★ Give up? Well, it's a flax spinning wheel and one of the oldest in America. It may look crude but it did the job!

19

★ An early 1800s mercury mirror in a walnut frame. Over the years the air dissolved the mercury, leaving a distorted vision. A true primitive of America!

★ "Potty," "Thunder-mug" — call it what you wiil — it beat going out into two feet of snow at ten degrees below zero. Usually, after it was used, the contents were poured into a larger container, kept beneath the wash stand. Lots of them are collectible today. The one shown is made of ironstone, about 1850.

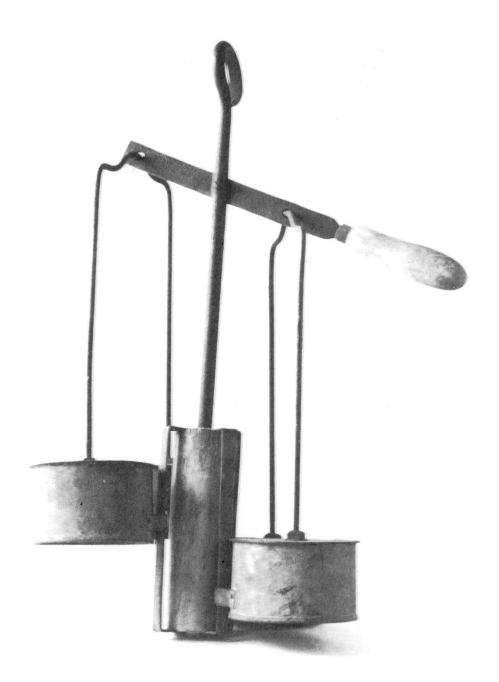

★ No, it's not an early cocktail shaker. If you guessed an early washing machine, operated by hand, go to the head of the tub. When you raised and lowered the handle, the metal caps jostled the wash. Early 1800s.

21

★ This cream churn was made in Georgia in the early 1800s. Earthenware, the "2" meant it was a two gallon job. Every home had one and many a boy went to bed with sore arm from pulling the dasher up and down for hours at a time.

★ These hooks were used for hanging kettles in the early American fireplaces.

★ A meal scoop, mid-1800s, used mostly in the granary or barn.

★ This primitive deeds box, lined with paper from an English book, dates to the early 1700s. It was leather bound with a crude lock. The frame of the box is of wood.

★ A delightful collection of hand-made keys, for every type of primitive cabinet, corner cupboard, what-have-you. Some are cast brass, others hand-forged from iron.

★ In the early homes of America the lock was on the inside of the door, thus requiring an extra long key. When not in use, it folded up so it could be carried more easily in one's pocket.

★ One of the earliest devices for chopping kale or cabbage in a wooden dough bowl, this item dates back to the mid-1800s and was used in every household until the 1900s.

★ This hand-made wooden keg was obviously used to hold spirits because of the bung on the side. The wooden wrappings are bands made of white oak. It has to be early 1800s. A beauty!

25

★ Gourds were grown to be used, not to be looked at. Two items you see here were used for dipping water from a bucket. The piece in the middle was a honey jug.

★ A meal sifter, it took the lumps out of flour before it reached the baking stage. Mid-1800s.

★ This tool, a closed scorp, was used to gouge out wood to make a dough bowl. It was sharpened from time to time but it was still a job to make a half-decent bowl without going through the bottom. Early 1820s.

★ Hilarious or not, what you're looking at is a mousetrap, the ingenious invention of a man who tired of hearing his wife say, "The mice have eaten the cheese again!" It probably worked or he wouldn't have made it. Just exactly where the mouse ended up is lost to history. Possibly in the soup pot!

27

★ A "rope key" or a "rope jack," this was used to tighten the ropes on a rope bed. Late 1700s.

★ The pioneer couldn't drive to the local tobacco store, so he rolled his own cigars and pressed them into shape in this hand-carved mold. Early 1800s. He grew the tobacco too!

★ Usually carved from maple or hickory, a wood that would withstand boiling fat or the heat of the fire, these early American ladles served hundreds of purposes.

★ One of the earliest types of candle snuffers. The wick was kept trimmed with this crude instrument. Early 1800s. if not earlier.

★ An example of a preserve jar, hand-made and fired in the ashes of the fire-place in the pioneer's cabin. Primitive and crude, it nevertheless did the job when a wooden plug was forced down in the top and surrounded by candle or bee's wax.

★ This wicker-covered whiskey jug was made for traveling. It didn't stay full very long but could always be re-filled. It dates back to the mid-1800s. Probably an import from England.

★ Often called "the housewife's savior," the dough bowl was as important to her as her husband's rifle and broad axe were to him. This bowl goes back to the early 1800s and is hand-carved from buckeye.

★ Kids are kids, whether it be in the 20th century or 200 years earlier. This crudely-made doll was the loving effort of a father who knew the loneliness of his children and, in his own way, tried to make their life a little easier. Mom probably added a homespun dress and a piece of lace, if she had any.

31

★ This kerosene lamp with two handles is of unusual design. Was it to attract buyers or increase safety of handling?

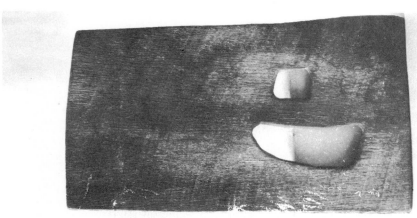

★ No, it's not an early painter's palette. It's a meal scoop, used to scoop flour grain from a box into a sack. It was whittled out by hand.

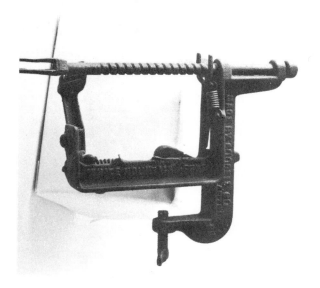

★ Though they're still made today by the same firm in New Hampshire, this apple peeler goes back to the 1800s.

★ "Swing your partner!" With one swig from this jug, you did just that! In the days when the Revenue agents weren't breathing down your back, it was considered a skillful trade to make White Lightning, Moonshine — call it what you will. It took a good man to take a good swig without falling down.

★ These just have to be the earliest can opener and cork screw around today. Before the mid-1800s.

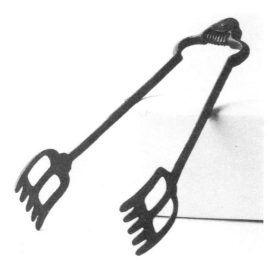

★ Coal tongs of the late 1800s — a much used item, you can be sure.

★ This is one of the earliest "store bought" locks in America. The plate swung down to keep water out of the keyhole when the lock was closed. Mid-to-late 1800s.

★ One of the earliest ink-wells known. It contained a mixture of soot, or bat's blood and water. These served well as an early form of ink.

★ This adjustable candleholder is dated 1840. The pioneers didn't waste wax!

★ A coffee grinder, pure and simple. All hand-made, it hung on the wall when not in use. Early 1800s.

★ This is a beeswax mold, used to make blocks of beeswax. This versatile product was used for waxing thread to make it stronger, and for all kinds of "water proofing" in the early 1800s. It looks like a cigar mold — but it isn't.

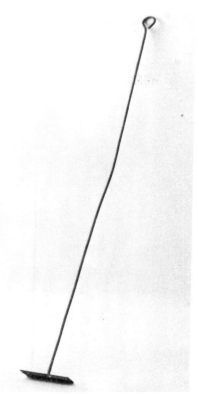

★ This simple gadget was used for a simple chore, cleaning the soot from the stove chimney, or from the narrow space above the oven of an old-fashioned kitchen range.

★ The top section of the nutmeg grater was used to store the nutmeg nuts. When the nut was grated, the contents came out of the hole at the bottom. Early 1900s.

★ This hand-carved chalk box was used in the early schoolhouse. The lid prevented the mice from getting at the chalk during the time the schoolmarm was away from the cabin-like building. Early 1800s.

★ Just two of the many kitchen utensils the farmer's wife had made, or bought from a traveling peddler. Late 1800s.

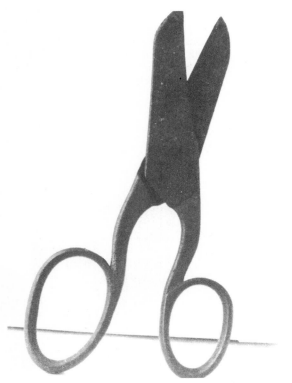

★ These crudely-made shears were used by the pioneer woman to snip the cloth or trim the home-spun.

★ This child's rocker, made from maple with a stripped white oak seat, was probably made by an adoring grandparent in the early 1800s. At one time the back might have had a piece of carpeting.

★ A wooden sausage mill, it was crude but it worked. Before the 1850s.

★ A scrub broom, made from one piece of hickory. It was used for scrubbing the puncheon floors of the cabins in the late 1700s and early 1800s.

★ A baby's highchair made with wooden pegs, hickory, early 1800s. A true labor of love!

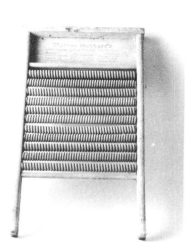 

★ Wash boards came in many sizes and shapes. Mother Hubbard's Standard shown here has wooden scrubbers; the other is brass plated. These two are late 1800 models. Earlier models were known as far back as the late 1700s.

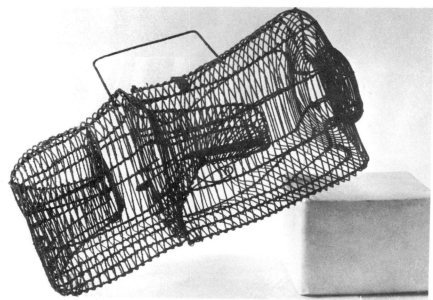

★ This is a crude mouse trap. When cheese was added, what mouse could resist! The handle was used to pick up the trap to carry it to the nearest creek where said mouse met his end by drowning.

41

★ By rubbing the two wooden paddles back and forth, the pioneer processed the wool or cotton preparatory to spinning. It's what they had and what they used. Mid-1800s.

The Pioneer Farm

★ A horse collar made from corn husks, late 1700s. They were cheap, but how long did they last?

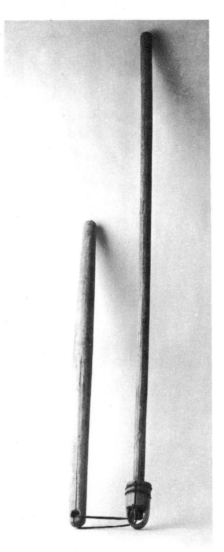

★ If you said "mallet," you're almost correct. The correct name is commander, used for splitting rails. Possibly Abe used this one on the way to the White House!

★ This is a flail and was used for threshing grain — "separating the wheat from the chaff" as it were. Early 1800s.

★ This pair of wrought iron barn hinges was made on a forge, hammered out to the particular shape desired by the pioneer farmer. This particular pair came from a barn that was built in 1805.

★ These grinding stones were made from sandstone and mounted on an axle. They were then cranked by hand or by foot pedals. A can of water dripped water to keep the stone wet while the axe sharpener did his work.

★ This is a linseed oil bucket, found in most barns in the mid-1800s. Most people mistake them for kerosene cans. They're not.

★ A half-bushel grain measure. Most farmers kept them in the barn by the grain bin. They go from the early 1700s right into the 20th century.

★ Hand-carved and hand-forged, this early 1800s pulley block eased the load when loading hay into the barn or pulling a wagon out of the mud.

★ Crudely-made block planes such as these were used to smooth the wood for making pie safes, dressers, beds, or whatever. Completely handcrafted, they did the job in the early 1800s. Today, they look great hanging from a mantlepiece.

★ This hand-forged spur was used on the frontier to train and control horses. The Spanish-type rowel, eight-pointed, let the horse know who was the boss!

★ This monstrous-looking device is a wire stretcher, used in the early days to tighten up fences.

★ This is a shoulder yoke, used for carrying pails of water, milk, or maple sap. Usually found in New England, mid-1800s.

★ This "rattletrap" or noise maker was used for having fun, but also for scaring crows out of the cornfield. Mid-1800s.

★ These early ice tongs were used when ice was cut from frozen lakes in the winter and stored in a barn, covered with sawdust to prevent melting in summer months. Mid-1800s and later.

★ These hand-made bells were hung around the neck of the cow or the sheep. Before the land was cleared, it was a chore to find the herd, especially if it ranged in woods or forest. The bell could be heard by the herdsman.

★ You're looking at one of the earliest forms of barbed wire, called "devil's wire" by the cattlemen who considered the range "open." The metal gadget stretched the wire tight between the posts.

★ This ominous looking instrument was fastened to a long handle and used to chisel ice.

★ One of the earliest forms of wooden clamps. Most farmhouses had them in the carpenter's shop. They were used with glue made from the shavings from a horse's hoof.

★ Hand-made wheel hubs, made from locust. When spokes and rim were added, you were in business. Early 1800s.

★ This is a winnowing tray, used for separating the chaff from the grain. Here again we find split white oak strips, woven into a pattern and placed in a wooden frame. Early 1800s.

★ Old wooden stirrups make serviceable napkin holders; or hang them on the wall for towel holders. These are quite old.

★ Called a "buttress," this was used for trimming the hooves of oxen in the early days.

★ A very early buck saw. It was used to cut thin pieces of lumber, and to fashion scroll work.

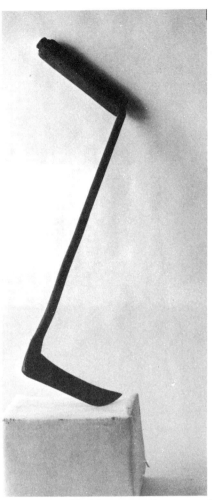

★ Called a "spud," this was used for peeling bark from trees or logs.

★ This handled instrument was used for cutting cane or sorghum about the time George Washington was crossing the Delaware.

★ A goat yoke, this contraption kept Billy from getting through the fence. The wood was bent to shape by soaking it in water, then placing it in a frame until dry. Mid-1800s.

★ This hand-made device is a cow weaner. Strapped around the cow's udder, it kept the cow from sucking herself after the calf had left for greener pastures.

★ Wanting the product of the honey bee and finding the tree were two different stories. First they caught a bee, put it in the box which had colored chalk in it. Then the bee was released and followed. Then another was caught and so on until the bee tree was found. Then the fun began!

★ This castiron hitching block was fastened to the horse's bridle by a snap hook, to keep the horse from leaving the scene while the owner was shopping or visiting with friends.

★ This calf weaner was clamped in the calf's nostrils. When the calf tried to take milk from the cow, mama kicked said calf into the next county. Mid-1800s.

★ This is an apple corer. It was hand-soldered by a tinsmith. It dates back to the mid-1800s.

★ Take a guess! Give up? Well, it's a hand-carved grease gun. When filled with bear grease, it was used to lubricate the wagon axles by pulling and pushing the plunger. Late 1700s.

★ Today they call the game of horseshoes "barnyard pool." In pioneer days, this hand-forged shoe would have been for a large mule or plow horse.

★ These crudely-carved initials made from dogwood were used to imprint letters in early type concrete. Pre-Civil War.

★ There were several kinds of calf weaners. This type was worn by the calf. As it tried to nurse, the pressure imbedded the sharp spurs in the calf's nose, discouraging it.

★ Home-made mule or horse bits came in all sizes. This one was probably made in the mid-to-late 1800s.

★ Hand-forged at the blacksmith's shop, this very early branding iron identified a man's horses and cows.

★ This grain sack is one of the earliest made on the frontier. When the grain was removed, Ma made a dress or petticoat from the sack.

★ An early two-prong hay fork, rare in this size and type.

★ Slip your finger through the leather loop and you're ready to husk corn. These were used for years all over America until machines replaced hand labor.

★ This early 1800s draw knife was used to make anything concave, such as a dough or fruit bowl. You placed the wood between your knees and pulled the blade toward you.

★ The difference between life and death on the frontier was a man's horse. He kept his livestock in prime condition if he wanted to survive. This horse curry comb would sell like crazy today, with some of the hairdos you see.

★ If you could find some-
one brave enough to hold
the patient, this instrument
was used to remove teeth
that had gone bad. It was
hand forged in a black-
smith's shop. Early 1800s.

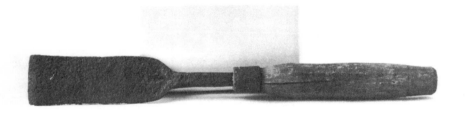

★ Just another example of the ability of the pioneer to make what he needed. This
heavy chisel was probably used to make mortise joints when building cabins of
the early 1800s.

★ This vicious-looking instrument was actually used for cutting corn in the field.
Obviously hand-made, it did the job and probably served other purposes.

★ Hand-made from first to last, this is an early form of a corn planter. The seed corn was put in the top and the bottom part was shoved into the ground at regular intervals. It goes back a long way.

★ This hand adze was used for smoothing timber, probably the first wooden floors ever used in the early cabins. It took a good man to use it from dawn to dusk!

★ This instrument was used to dig gingseng, an herb with a thick, aromatic root. Today the root sells for around $45 a pound — when one can find it! Our "digger" goes back to the mid-1800s.

★ It looks like a hay bale hook but it was used to drag the hog from where it was killed to the scalding pot. Early 1800s.

★ This was called a "froe," and was used in the days when the pioneers made wooden shingles by hand. Early 1800s.

★ This was called a wheelwright's reamer and was used for enlarging hub holes on wagon wheels.

67

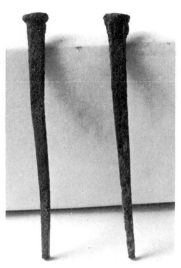

★ The earliest form of nails, these came from the ruins of the Jamestown (Virginia) colony. They were entirely forged by hand. Little wonder in those days the pioneers burned down the old building just to get the nails to erect a new building.

★ Made of strips of white oak, soaked in water to make the wood easier to work with, this is a mule muzzle.

★ The bee smoker is still used today. When you want to remove honey from the hive, you place an oily rag in the round container, light it, then pump the bellows. Usually it works. If it doesn't, you can always run like . . . well, you run!

★ This broad axe was used for splitting logs, or hewing logs to their proper shape. Almost as important as the pioneer's rifle, it was in continuous use until the late 1800s.

★ This is a hand adze of the mid-1800s.

★ This early American ladle was used to dip pine tar or pitch from a bucket to grease wagon axles.

Tools of Trade

★ This portable horse-shoeing kit held the tools necessary for shoeing "Old Dobbin." The boxes at the top held the horseshoe nails. Today, they make fine magazine racks.

★ A hand-made saw — goodness knows what it was used for. But, it's very old, dating back to the early 1800s.

★ Spoke shave — used to make wagon spokes for carriages, stage coaches, farm wagons, etc. Used in mid-1800s.

★ This was a tire puller, used to pull the iron rims on the wooden wagon wheels. Early 1800s.

★ Called a "traveler," this instrument was used by a blacksmith to measure the distance around a wooden wagon wheel so he could forge an iron rim to the exact size. Wagons didn't go far over rough, unpaved trails without iron-rimmed wheels.

73

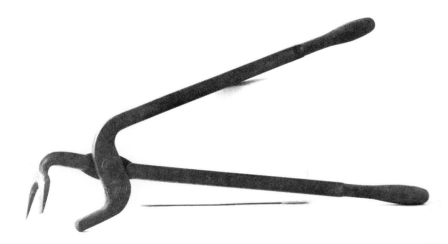

★ These are blacksmith's tongs. Their specific purpose is not known to this writer. Help!

★ Early blacksmith tools with the usual leather apron. They were important in the heyday of the horse, mule, and ox. Early 1800s.

★ This pair of calipers was used by a blacksmith to measure the thickness of wagon hubs, etc. Early 1800s.

★ This device was used to cut the end of a wagon spoke, the part that fitted up next to the rim. Adjustable, it could be used for several size spokes. It dates back to the early 1800s.

★ This was one of the earliest forms of the circular saw, going back to the 1600s. It was operated by a spring pole, a rope, and a foot treadle — a darned good way to lose a hand if you didn't know what you were doing!

★ This hand-made plane was "adjustable" and was used to carve moldings for corner cupboards, ceilings, staircases, etc. The wood is cherry or maple and the cutting blade was hand-forged. Mid-1800s.

★ This is a hand drill from around 1800 that had many uses. It could bore through wood or leather. You'll see few pieces as old as this. This pioneer could make just about anything when he put his mind to it.

77

★ This "sled" auger was used for boring holes in cabin beams. A wooden peg was driven into the hole. Probably used for other types of drilling but the above was its chief use.

★ This draw knife was originally called a "draft shave" and was used to shape beams, spokes, and wooden pegs in the early 1800s.

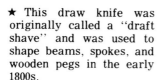

★ You'll seldom see an earlier brace and bit. It was made in Sheffield, England, and was brought to America in the 1840s. It was an invaluable instrument when it came to carpentry.

★ Hand-forged at the anvil, this bit was used to drill the holes in ship's planks or in large wooden structures. It dulled easily, and took a lot of manpower to force it to penetrate hard wood.

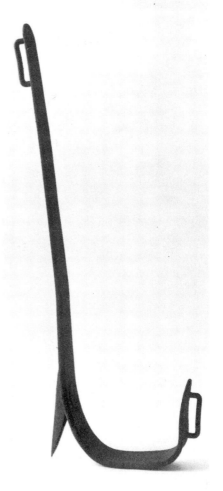

★ An early form of "tree climbers," they were used in the mid-1800s by lumberjacks to scale the big pines in the Northwest. They strapped to the leg with thick leather straps.

★ This is a peavey, used by lumbermen to roll heavy logs to the river's edge or onto a horse-drawn wagon. Its handle would have been about 6 feet long. Mid-1800s.

★ Two of these giant clamps were fastened to the rims of a wagon wheel; then poles were inserted in the U-shaped area to roll logs up onto the wagon. Early 1800s.

★ This is a hand-hewn cog wheel from an early grist mill, probably around 1820.

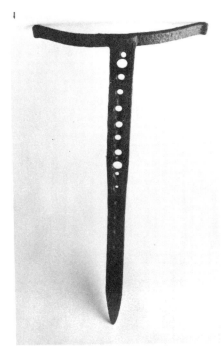

★ These are old mining picks shown without the handles. They were used in mines throughout America in the mid-1800s. Made of hand-forged iron, they had short handles so that the miner could dig out the coal, even in a kneeling position.

★ Made of hand-forged iron, it's called a breast plate. The different holes took different-sized drills, to be used in coal mines for drilling out coal. Very, very old!

★ A logging chain with hook, used to "snake" huge logs out of the forest with an eight-team oxen rig.

★ This is one of the earliest forms of weighing scales. One hook hung from a tree or beam while the other hook held the item to be weighed. Then the pear-shaped weight was moved back and forth until the long rod was on an even horizontal level. Early 1800s.

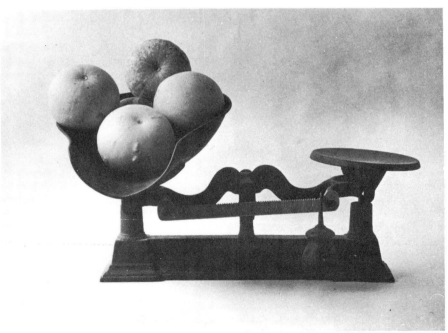

★ A cast-iron scale from an old grocery store. See what you can do, decoration-wise, with primitives!

★ This ingenious device was a clamp
used by cobblers for holding leather
as they carved out the sole of a boot
or a strap for a horse's harness. Pressure on the lever kept the clamp tight.

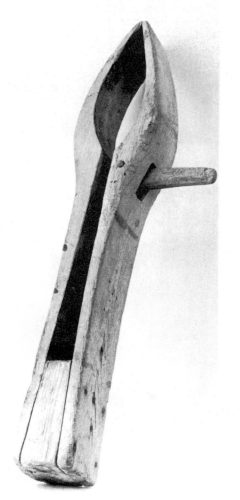

★ In early pioneer days when shoe
and boot soles were fastened to the
uppers with chestnut pegs, this tool
was used to go into the shoe or boot
to file off the sharp tips of wooden pegs.

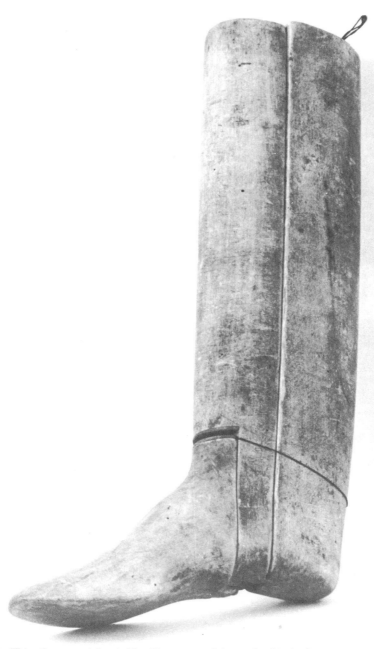

★ This three-part boot "last" was used to make boots for anyone who needed them. It was a product of the early 1800s. The cobbler carved out a last to fit your foot and leg, then kept the last in stock, come the time you needed a new pair of boots.

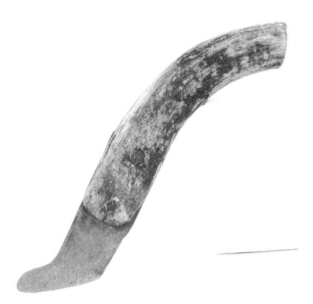

★ This crudely-made tool was used by a cobbler to cut through cow or horse hide, preparatory to making shoes, aprons, etc.

★ This is a "flambeau," or flaming torch, used by railroad men to light their way when checking the wheels, pistons, and other parts of the early wood-burning railroad engines. Coal oil, put in at the top, dripped down onto the cloth wick. Many a trainman scorched his britches when he got careless with the flame!

★ An elaborate form of the railroad flambeau, used for lighting the railroadman's way when inspecting his engine and cars. Mid-1800s.

★ This is a crude, castiron mortar and pestle, used for crushing rock, possibly to extract gold. It could still be used.

★ We don't claim to know everything. If you know what this is, tell us! Probably used by a carpenter or a cabinetmaker.

★ With an iron head, this tool was used to crush rocks for making roads, or any surface that had to be hard and solid enough to take the weight of heavily-loaded wagons.

88

Family, Recreational, Miscellany

★ This wooden mortar and pestle would have to go back to late 1700s or early 1800s. Everyone in the area "doctored" the patient. If you took some of the frog's leg, spider web, lizard tail remedies that were guaranteed to work you were lucky to escape alive.

★ This beaverskin tophat was worn for weddings, funerals, any festive occasions in the mid-1800s.

★ Shoes! Go without them for one day, then know what your ancestors suffered through. The pair on the left has soles fastened on with chestnut pegs; the other pair is handsewn. They squeaked in dry weather, floated on your feet in wet weather, and in general were ill-fitting.

★ Entirely made by hand, great great grandma's bonnet kept her from getting sunstroke while hoeing her tobacco or vegetable patch.

★ Ladies of genteel background used this side saddle when it was necessary to ride any distance. One leg hooked over the post, the other foot slipped into the stirrup. Pre-Civil War, entirely hand-made, with a design stitched in the leather.

★ These fluting irons were used for putting pleats in bonnets and skirts in the early-to-mid-1800s. Probably also used for recurling wigs in the same period.

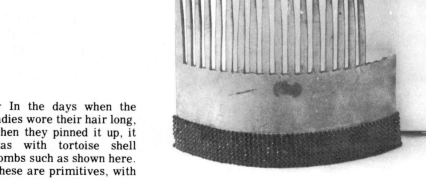

★ In the days when the ladies wore their hair long, when they pinned it up, it was with tortoise shell combs such as shown here. These are primitives, with no ornate jewels or carvings. Early 1800s.

★ Though these are modern, they're exact duplicates of the dried apple head doll with corn shuck bodies. Every piece is hand-crafted by the mountain people of the Appalachias.

★ The crudest form of a baby's rattle, it did the job. The jingle-jangle kept baby occupied while mom went about her chores. Early 1800s.

★ These are turkey calls made from the wing bone of a turkey. It took a good man to bring a gobbler close enough for a shot. Early 1800s.

★ This is a hand-made banjo that probably used catgut for strings. It worked, and many a dancer "swung his partner" to its tune.

★ If you are a fox, start running! This is one of the earliest types of foxhorns, carved from pine. When blown properly, you could hear it a mile away. Probably from the early 1800s.

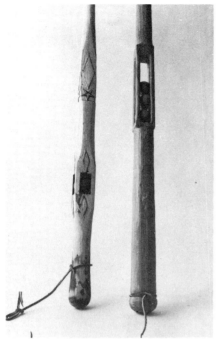

★ Whittling was a way of life in the early days of America. The two novelty items shown here are typical examples.

★ This early banjo's "head" was made from catgut. It lasted a long time.

★ A man with a weak wrist was in bad shape when it came to chopping down trees or lifting heavy weights. These wrist supports from the early 1800s helped. Without them more than one man would have gone broke because he couldn't lift his weight in the logging camps.

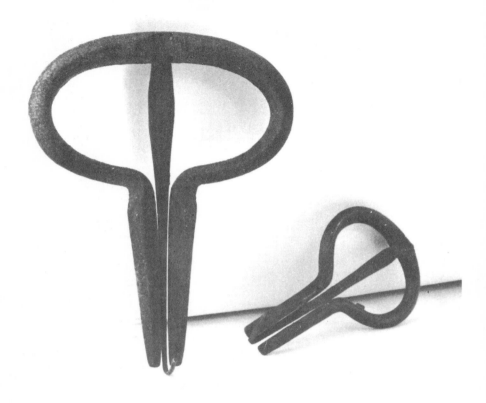

★ These early hand-crafted Jew's harps still play. Many a square dance started when someone brought out one of these.

★ One of the earliest razors ever found, it has a wooden handle. If it was itchy to grow a beard, think what one went through to remove same!

★ "Health" tonics have been around for centuries. This particular brand contained 10 percent alcohol, which was enough to keep grandpa going when grandma had hidden his favorite jug.

★ This is an early razor hone, hand-made.

★ Came the end of the day, father needed something to remove his boots with. This is hand-carved and goes back to the early 1800s.

★ In days gone by, people in the rural areas bought many items by mail. Often shoes didn't fit. If father had a bunion, this instrument was used to go up into the toe area of the boot (or shoe) and, with a little pressure, space was widened for relief.

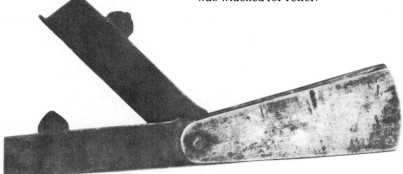

★ Call it a phlebotome or a fleam, it was a blood letter, used in the early days when one believed that the bad blood settled in the neck and had to be removed when the pains set in. Early 1800s, until we wised up and went to real doctors.

★ Ouch! When the nearest dentist was 50 miles away, dad did his own tooth pulling. That's what this is — an early tooth puller.

★ These saddle bags, tanned by hand and hand-sewn, carried the post mail over many a mountain trail. You can just barely see the "U.S." at the top of the middle strap, indicating that at one time they were used by a cavalry unit.

★ When a man smashed his finger but still had to work to support his family, he used this crude "finger protector," hand - made from metal chain links. Early 1800s.

★ One of the earliest pack saddles known, it was probably used on a donkey's back to carry supplies into the mining camps in the mid-1840s in the gold fields of California.

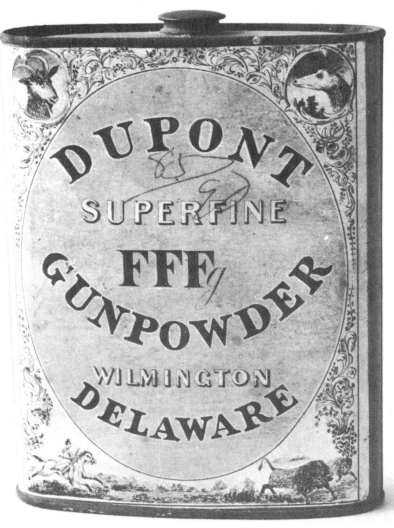

★ When you loaded your own shells, this is the gunpowder you used. Black powder, when it got wet, then dried, was dangerous. Mid-1800s.

★ This instrument was used to "seat" the primer cap when loading your own shotgun shells. If you squeezed too hard, look out! It was used around the Civil War before cheap ammunition came on the market.

★ Both bullet molds shown here are of the earliest and crudest design. One is made entirely of wood. Back in the 1700s, a man without minnie balls or lead shot for his "Betsy" didn't last too long on the frontier.

★ This instrument did one thing — it reloaded the old brass shells the pioneer used to bring down game for his family's table. Once a month, if he was lucky, he went to the fort to purchase gunpowder, primers, and pieces for his long rifle that needed replacing.

★ This powder flask was made from a cow's horn, with a wooden plug at the top and straps to carry it over your shoulder. Dating back before the Revolution, every pioneer relied on God, dry powder, and a steady aim.

★ These three objects were used for measuring gunpowder in the days when, if you put too much into the barrel, BOOM! Early 1800s.

103

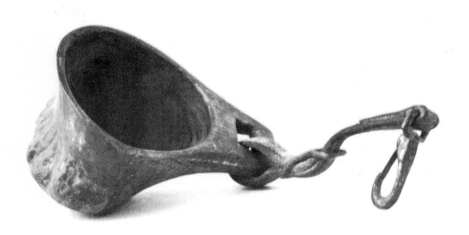

★ This drinking cup, carved from the burl of a walnut tree, hung from the saddle of a Post Rider. When thirsty, he dipped the cup into a nearby stream. Early 1800s.

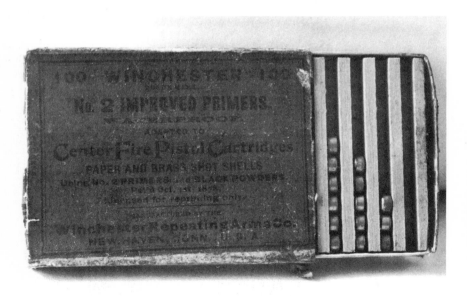

★ In the days when you reloaded your own shells, the primer cap was all-important. Winchester made caps, as did Colt and Remington. Mid-1800s.

★ This ball-and-cap single shot pistol and powder pouch, adjustable to give two different measures of powder, date back to the early 1800s.

★ A hand-made bear trap, dating back to the mid-1700s.

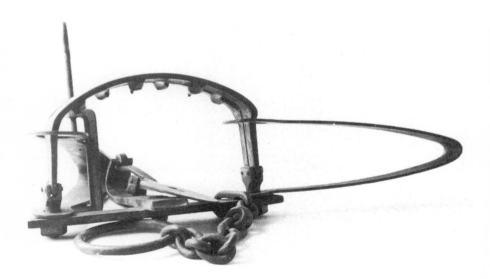

★ This huge bear trap is over six feet long and can only be cocked by screwing down the hinge at one side. It was chained to a tree and baited with a dead rabbit or a piece of deer meat. Mid-1800s.

★ The pioneers lived off the land. This dried coonskin is an indication of just that. When curing, the stench would drive a buzzard off a gut cart; but the fur was used for making sleigh robes and many other useful items. What pioneer boy didn't wear a cap with a coonskin tail hanging down the back?

★ This is an early form of fishhook. When cocked and the fish swam into it — Zap! Mid-1800s. Illegal in most states today.

★ This is not really a primitive, but in this day and age the ball and chain of the chain gang should be primitive in any state!

★ When the High Sheriff placed these on your wrists (or ankles) there was no place to go but to jail. Early 1800s.